Parody and Pastiche in Bill Kohn's *Udaipur Tinsmiths*

Robert E. Kohn

Professor Emeritus of Economics

Southern Illinois University Edwardsville

Parody and Pastiche in *Udaipur Tinsmiths*

Copyright © 2014 by Robert E. Kohn

All rights reserved

First Edition Printed by Createspace 2014

ISBN-13: 978-1495480508

ISBN-10: 149548050X

Front and back cover designs by Joel M. Kohn

Front cover image: Bill Kohn, *Udaipur Tinsmiths*, 1964, oil on canvas, 47" x 55 ½"

Book formatted by Joel M. Kohn

DEDICATION

I dedicate this book to Bill Kohn's wife, Pat, and children, Joshua and Sophie, whose encouragement has been invaluable.

TABLE OF CONTENTS

	Figure 1. *Udaipur Tinsmiths* grid	i
	Prologue	1
Chapter 1	Ambiguity in Art by Arthur Mange	2
Chapter 2	Clement Greenberg	9
Chapter 3	Paul A. Samuelson	16
	Figure 2. Samuelson's letter page 1	18
	Figure 3. Samuelson's letter page 2	19
Chapter 4	Andreas Huyssen	20
	Epilogue	24

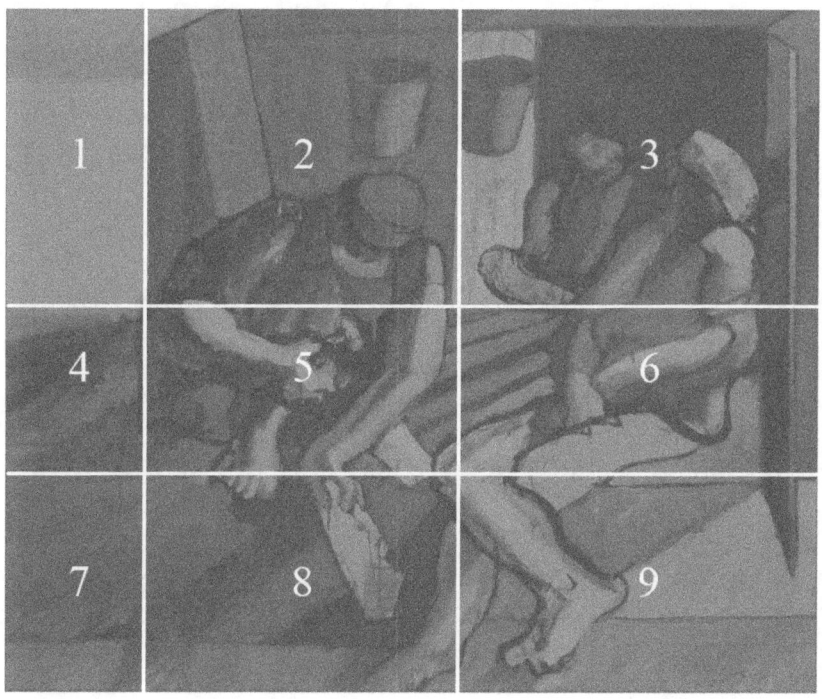

Figure 1. Subdivision *of Udaipur Tinsmiths* into Nine Panels for Locating Examples of Bill Kohn's Pastiche and Parody

PROLOGUE

On January 20, 2014, I was discharged from Barnes Jewish Hospital after a week of treatment for septic shock complicated by metastatic prostate cancer. My prognosis is uncertain and I am anxious to bring my interpretation of my brother's painting *Udaipur Tinsmiths* to full fruition while I am able. I believe that the story of this painting is important, and there may even be lessons in that story. To my pleasant surprise, Bill's close friend from early childhood, Arthur Mange, volunteered his thoughts, in the form of a letter, on the importance of ambiguity in art.

CHAPTER 1. AMBIGUITY IN ART
BY ARTHUR MANGE

160 Gray Street
Amherst, MA 01002

December 14, 2013

If I didn't say before, you are welcome to use my letters as you will. But what do I know? For I am not at all an art critic with any real knowledge of the subject. But if you need to refer to my credentials, I am a good black and white photographer with some two dozen more-or-less local shows (some juried, some not). You can see a sample of my work at pvphotoartists.org and click on Members' Online Galleries. Also for 14 years I have helped run a community art gallery, the Burnett Gallery at the Jones Library in Amherst. (Google joneslibrary.org and click on Programs/Burnett Gallery.)

Good luck with your new *Tinsmiths* paper.

Arthur

Parody and Pastiche in Bill Kohn's *Udaipur Tinsmiths*

160 Gray Street
Amherst, MA 01002

December 14, 2013

Dear Bob,

Having read [your book] *A Darwinian Reading of Bill Kohn's Painting*, which Franklin [i.e., Arthur's older brother] brought to my attention, I feel behooved to say something about it.

A lot of the book is beyond my experience – modernism vs postmodernism – the interpretation of cave art and the role of shamans– and much else, and I say little about those things. On the other hand, I can see the tinsmiths as well as anyone else. So here goes.

I label the muscular tinsmith with the hammer #1, the one on the right with his hands in his crotch #2, and the receding one against the black panel as #3.

As you emphasize, we see a mix of representational and abstract art. The abstract aspects include the puzzling planes of the shack, the platform, and the foreground areas. It is hard to know with assurance where some surfaces actually exist in space and even what is vertical and what is horizontal. Bill was having fun and must have mused, "I'll leave that to the viewer." I am reminded of a *New Yorker* cartoon of men high up among the steel beams of a building under construction. The beams cross each other in literally impossible positions. One workman shouts to the ground: "Escher! Get your ass up here."

The figures, too, are both representational and abstract in color and shape. My interpretation of #1 is that he is hitting a nail into a 2x4, the nail being held between his left thumb and index finger pretty much as one would hold a nail for hitting. You note that the hand holding the nail (if that is what it is doing) is the most realistic part of the painting. I don't see a nail there, but on the other hand, I don't see the nails on which the pails hang either. Does Bill suppose that the viewer will add these three nails? The hammer is held somewhat awkwardly—not in a proper position.

But the main puzzle to me about #1 (and you speak to this) is, Where is the tinsmith's left leg? It should be represented sort of like the right one if he is squatting. I cannot imagine the left leg being hidden behind him. Anatomy just doesn't allow that. His right hip is resting solidly on the platform and so must be his left hip – they are solidly attached to each other after all. Possibly the undefined left foot, if that is what it is, is a prosthetic, and he has no left leg at all. Does that make sense? A one-legged tinsmith? Why not?

A related puzzle is that the 2x4, if that is what it is, seems to be

Parody and Pastiche in Bill Kohn's *Udaipur Tinsmiths*

floating in space where one could hardly be hammering a nail into it effectively. Perhaps (1) #1 is sitting on the other end of the 2x4 (uncomfortably), or (2) the red paint area backing up the wood (with darker slashing areas) is actually a horizontal plane—an extension of the bluish area where the tinsmith sits, or (3) Bill means to suggest something mystical in the unseen support of the 2x4. Your guess is as good as mine. I think Bill is playing with his viewers, allowing multiple interpretations, which you mention several times in your book.

It is a decent guess that the tan panel behind the tinsmith is a sheet of tin. It is the right size and color to make into a pail, but of course, it is not the right shape, which would have to be curved a bit. What is the dark brownish, smudgy cloak-like thing above the right shoulder and upper arm, extending below the elbow and forearm? We know that Bill was a fine craftsman and could make anything look like it is. Why is he being obtuse? Is he playing to critics and/or trend-setters? I really don't know what abstract art is all about, to tell you the truth.

So that's not the biggest puzzle to me. Why does #2 have *his* (he looks male to me) hands in his crotch, and what are those two little triangles, which to me seem out of place with the otherwise mostly curvy figures? Perhaps the triangles are marks or tears in his pants. That seems unlikely but no more so than fingertips as you suggest, but who knows? Maybe the triangles are abstract spear points, which allude to your thesis of the passage of cave artist genes (through a hundred generations or more) to Bill. And they are so close to #2's reproductive parts! I'm getting carried away here. But wait ...

Since the painting invites ambiguity, I note that I can see a fourth person (#4) in the picture, a viewpoint that came about because I can't believe that #2's right upper arm (painted tannish) really articulates with his shoulder, which seems to be hidden by his beard. (Given that #1 doesn't seem to have a left leg at all, perhaps I should not be surprised that #2's right arm doesn't connect.) Rather, I see another person (sex unknown) who is facing #2—face to face but a little behind—with lighter-colored skin on the back of the neck, and mostly hidden by #2. It is #4's (properly connected) right arm that extends easily into the crotch of #2. I would say that this is supported by the fact that the clothes over the left and right arms (if they both belonged to #2) are different, except, as you note, the clothes on the arms of #1 are different too. Most peculiar. Getting even sexier, does #2 have a large erection under the bulge in #2's purple shirt (extending into the tannish area of the right arm of #2 – or #4)? Could Bill have this in mind as a possible interpretation? Certainly not proper public comportment.

As for Darwinian interpretations of Bill's work, sure, there is no reason not to ascribe Bill's talent, at least in part, to genes, perhaps to those of cave artists, which he possibly inherited in goodly measure.

Parody and Pastiche in Bill Kohn's *Udaipur Tinsmiths*

Artistic talent might be sexually selected. It is easy enough to imagine that cave artists and later artisans could draw female admirers. And the reverse for female artists. (This is certainly a testable hypothesis.) We should not forget, however, that large genetic influences do not rule out large environmental influences. Bill had good teachers and access to an arty world (including visits to a stunning cave art), in the absence of which, he might not have grown up to be a famous painter. We were in an art class together taught by a Miss Tedman (?) at about age ten in the basement of Bixby at the corner of Skinker and Forsyth. He discovered, or already knew, that he was artistically talented (and I was not). (Environmental and genetic influences likely interact with each other.) I cannot point you to an academic treatise on the genetic aspects of artistic talent (but I could dig one out if you like), but generally most behavioral traits are influenced about 50:50 (or 60:40 or 40:60) by genetic inheritance versus environmental experiences. This would include mathematical, musical, and artistic talent as well as different aspects of intelligence and personality.

One can hardly spend so much time reading your comments about the *Udaipur Tinsmiths*, and replying to your comments, inadequately I fear, without being taken with the painting itself. It really has grown into me with all its mysteries, which, we will never solve. Thanks for your book which you signed (for the bookstore sales).

Cheers,

p.s. 1: Feel free to share this letter if you wish. I am sending a copy to Franklin.

p.s. 2: I have several of Bill's paintings and, perhaps a half dozen drawings, if I can find them all. One is a watercolor Mexican church from 1978 hanging above our computer, and there are three sketches from India from 1965 and 1966 that hang in one horizontal frame above our fireplace (and partly in the style of your figure 5). Are the particulars of any interest to you? Is there a catalog of Bill's work? Can I have your e-mail address? Mine is amange@bio.umass.edu
I did read the article by Greenberg, but it was too much for me. Was there a suggestion that artists should do what he thought they should do? Presumptuous?

I had one further thought about the triangular shapes on #2's thigh. Might they be the tips of a small tin snips hidden between his legs? That makes more scene-sense than anything else that we have conjured up. Bill could have drawn them more realistically, of course, but he also could have drawn real nails too (in the 2x4 perhaps and supporting the two pails for sure) but he didn't. You know Bill's temperament better than I, but it seems he might have been playing with his viewers.

CHAPTER 2. CLEMENT GREENBERG

At my request, Arthur read Clement Greenberg's "Post Painterly Abstraction," pages 192-197 of *Clement Greenberg: The Collected Essays and Criticism: Volume 4 Modernism with a Vengeance: 1957-1969. Edited by John O'Brian*. Chicago: Chicago UP, 1995. Arthur was surely correct that Greenberg believed "that artists should do what he thought they should do?" which I strongly agree with Arthur was *"Presumptuous"* on Greenberg's part (My emphasis.) As Brian put it in the Foreword to Volume 4:

> Greenberg's formulations were read as close to an ultimatum. The rhetoric in which he touched his ideas seemed to allow little room for argument; either artists accepted the logic of his rationale or they risked producing "minor" work. [...] If art was to engage constantly in an enterprise of self criticism in order to remain uncontaminated, Greenberg understood that this amounted, as he said, to a form of "self-definition with a vengeance" (John O'Brian, xv).

There was no way that Greenberg would allow the kind of contaminated expression that Arthur Mange read into Bill's version of modern art. As a result, Greenberg rendered art "less imaginatively fulfilled than in the past" (O'Brian xv).

Robert E. Kohn

In *Udaiper Tinsmiths*, my brother struck back at Greenberg's arbitrary and narrow focus on Modernist Art, which he took to be an attack on his own aesthetics. Who gave Greenberg the exclusive authority to define the parameters of Modernist Art? In my book *A Darwinian Reading of Bill Kohn's Painting*, I suggest that Bill used pastiche to convey his displeasure with Greenberg's "self-definition with a vengeance" (O'Brian xv). Pastiche, as Bill used it, is best explained by Fredric Jameson in his essay "Postmodernism and Consumer Society," which is featured in *The Anti-Aesthetic: Essays on Postmodern Culture: Edited by Hal Foster,* Port Townsend: Bay Press, 1983:

> One of the most significant features or practices in postmodernism today is pastiche. I must first explain this term, which people generally tend to confuse with or assimilate to that related verbal phenomenon called parody. Both pastiche and parody involves the imitation or, better still, the mimicry of other styles and particularly the mannerisms and stylistic twitches of other styles. (Frederick Jameson 113).

Bill's *Udaipur Tinsmiths* is dense with patches of pastiche and parody. If they are harsh on Greenberg, Mange has shown that they are barbarous on Bill's own postmodern grotesqueries. His postmodern mimicry, first discovered in my *Darwinian Reading of Bill Kohn's Painting*, together with the mimicry of Greenberg's modernism, makes *Udaipur Tinsmiths* one of Bill's most interesting and important

Parody and Pastiche in Bill Kohn's *Udaipur Tinsmiths* paintings.

Bill's parody can be divided into three phases: Modernist, Postmodernist and Hypermodernist, some of which may overlap. It may even be useful to locate them graphically. The can of paint with three lines of drips against a white background on the left edge of panel 3 in Figure 1 appears to be a parody of the pails of paint that Morris Louis poured on canvases that he gravitationally maneuvered, as suggested by the downward slanting rivulets of paint along the vertical white line separating panels 5 and 6 of figure 1. The left thigh of the tinsmith on the right, along the bottom of panel 6, which connects to the balance of that thigh at the top of panel 9, is actually raw canvas with paint dripping downward: a parody of the Jackson Pollock paintings that Greenberg promoted. Panel 1 of Figure 1 is suggestive of the raw canvas on which Pollock dripped his paint. On the left side of *Udaipur Tinsmiths* and wrapping around below the central tinsmith are parodies suggestive of the color fields of Helen Frankenthaler (panel 4), of Mark Rothko (panel 7), and of Barnett Newman (panel 8). In contrast to the implied precision of these abstract expressionist icons, there are Bill's parodies of the postmodern fantastic, which Arthur Mange has fortuitously discovered for us in *Udaipur Tinsmiths*. These include the mismatched feet at the bottom of panel 5 and the missing knee below the head in panel 2. The pail is such an important symbol of Abstract Expressionism in *Udaipur Tinsmiths* that one wonders if the tinsmith's cap in panel 2 had special significance for Bill. The possibility that

that tinsmith, with his wide mustache, represents Bill may say something cerebral, as opposed to gravitational, about Morris Louis's artistic imagery.

I learned about Hypermoderism from the writing of Paul Virilio and accordingly attributed its ominousness to scientific and technological horrors. Now that I realize that Andreas Huyssen had Clement Greenberg in mind when he alluded to postmodern repudiation, I identify Hypermodernism with Greenberg's ultimate version of Abstract Expressionism that goes by the name of Post Painterly Abstraction. How my brother must have resented the idea of the *Post* Painterly, especially given its elegant connection by Greenberg

> to the formal qualities of Baroque art that separate it from High Renaissance or Classical art. Painterly means, among other things, the blurred, broken, loose definition of color and contour. The opposite of painterly is clear, unbroken, and sharp definition. (Clement Greenberg 192).

Early in my *Darwinian Reading of Bill Kohn's Painting*, I recognized the strong element of drawing in Udaipur Tinsmtiths, which I thought was derived from Julian Jaynes's *Origin of Consciousness in the Breakdown of the Bicameral Mind*. This shows how surprised I later was to see all the connections in Bill's painting to the Greenberg phenomenon. Bill must have bitterly counteracted with his strong pastiches of the painterly, especially in panels 3, 5, 6 and 9 of Figure 1. Abstract Expressionism was rooted in abstraction and painterliness, but still Greenberg could deny the latter a place in his Hypermodern scheme of firm contours, could even "claim—on the basis of experience alone—that openness and clarity are more conducive to freshness in abstract painting at this particular moment than most other instrumental qualities are—just as twenty years ago density and compactness were" (Greenberg 196).

In "Post Painterly Abstraction," Greenberg notes that some of the artists in the post painterly "exhibition look 'hard-edged,' but this by itself does not account for their inclusion" (196). The 2 by 4 in Panel 8, that causes Mange to marvel that it could be hammered into in the absence of firm support, in fact has a dark blue hard-edge that goes back behind that tinsmith's left thumb, well into Panel 5 . Bill had no compunctions against assuming properties for hard-edges. In contrast Greenberg waffled: hard-edges "are included because they have won their 'hardness' from the 'softness' of Painterly Abstraction; they have not inherited it from Mondrian, the Bauhaus, Suprematism, or anything else that came before" (Greenberg 196). How could Greenberg, or even the artists themselves, have known when and where they were first attracted to a particular aesthetic?

What we have here are two thrusts of modernism, the earlier and less rigorous, Painterly Abstraction, the later and more rigorous, Post Painterly Abstraction. Greenberg credits the latter with high keying, as well as lucidity of their color. They have a tendency, many of them, to stress contrasts of pure hue rather than contrasts of light and dark. For the sake of these, as well as in the interests of optical clarity, they shun thick paints and tactile effects. Some of them dilute their paint to an extreme and soak it into unsized and unprimed canvas. (Clement Greenberg 196).

Though the left arm of the tinsmith in Panel 2 and Panel 5 is painterly and drawn, there are still nice contrasts of pure hue as well as of light and dark. The same holds for the legs of the tinsmith in Panels 6 and 7. It's as though Bill is intensifying his repudiation of the more extreme hypermodernism in Figure 1. As for the thick paints and tactile effects that the Post Painterly Expressionists shunned, they are crucial in the faces of the three (possibly four) tinsmiths in Panels 2 and 3 of Figure 1. Returning to Greenberg's text:

In their reaction against the "hand-writing" and "gestures" of Painterly Abstraction, these artists also favor a relatively anonymous execution. (...) These artists prefer trued and faired edges simply because they call less attention to themselves as drawing—and by doing that they also get out of the way of color. (Clement Greenberg 197).

Because the tinsmith's face in Panel 2 could be Bill's, it is hardly anonymous. Anonymity is not what Bill is striving for. The thirty-one artists that Greenberg included in his 1964 exhibition were, he thought, "among the best new painters, but it does not include all of these. Even if it did it would still not be a show of 'the best new painters.' Thirty-one is simply too large a number for that" (196). It attests to his parsimony that Greenberg inclined to restrict the number of best new painters.

CHAPTER 3. PAUL A. SAMUELSON

I am hardly the first person to accuse Greenberg of biased scholarship. His editor, John O'Brian, reiterated a charge that Greenberg had structured the 1964

> exhibition to assert a personal notion of style; that is, to reveal what in his opinion the major ambitious art after Abstract Expressionism *ought to look like* and what means it *ought to employ* to gain this look. (O'Brian 196).

I was fortunate to learn about unbiased scholarship from Paul A. Samuelson, the first American to win the Nobel Prize in economics. I wrote to him several times, and though he would have had no reason to recognize my name or associate it with any thing I had written, he always replied. The most generous reply, because it contained original work on his part, is the letter of January 7, 1987, reproduced below, written in response to my "Optimal Quantity of a Controversial Good or Service," published in *Public Choice* 51.1 (1986).

At no point in the letter did Samuelson show disrespect for the junior professor I was, but was more inclined to criticize his own thoughts as over-hasty and tentative. He was willing to take a new tack, entirely different than the Pareto optimality that he is known for, and build on the frontier of Musgrave's thoughts. The concept of an "Ethical Function" of individual utility functions sounds promising, and I regret that Samuelson is no longer here to advocate for it.

Samuelson's economics have relevance to Modernism, Postmodernisn and Hypermodernism in the arts. Because of Greenberg's narrow purview of the modernisms, and the harms that it inflicted on my brother's artistic aspirations I am the more inclined to postmodernism. Yet, when I go back in time to the 1970s and 1980s, when I was an economist, I recall my own narrow policy purviews and recognize in myself the weaknesses I attribute to Greenberg. I am able, all the more, to admire Samuelson as a genuine postmodern thinker.

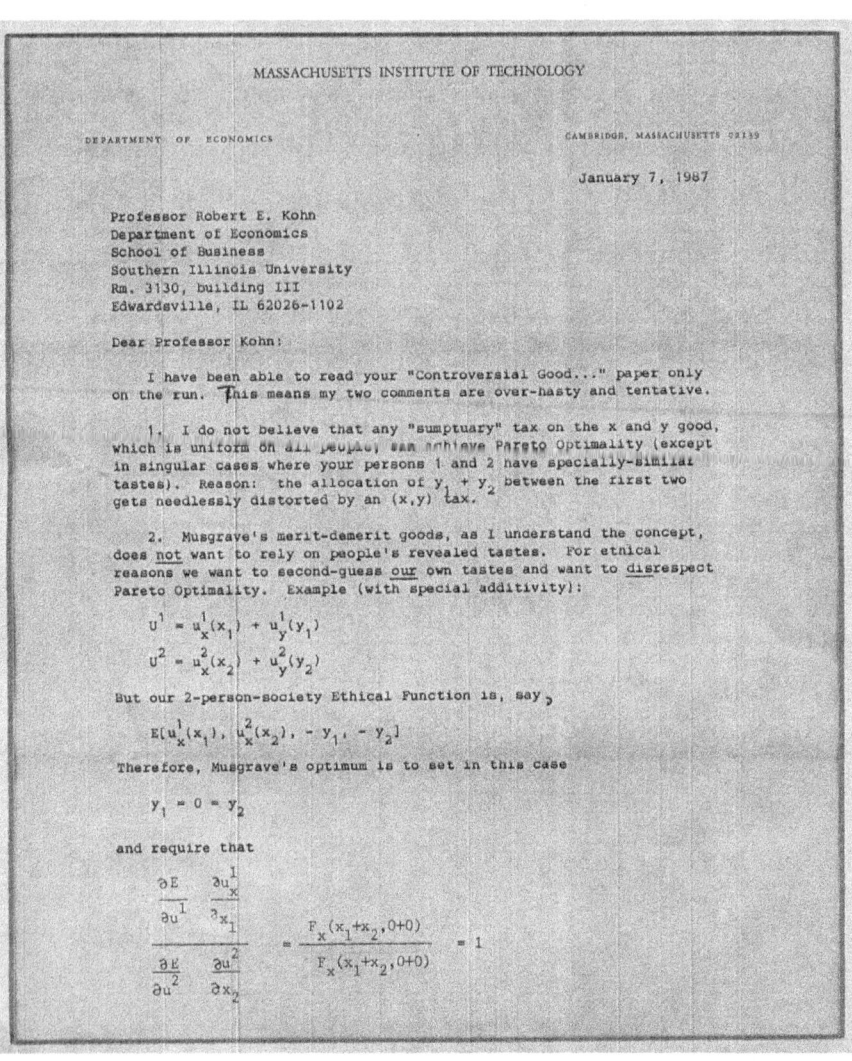

Figure 2. Samuelson's letter page 1

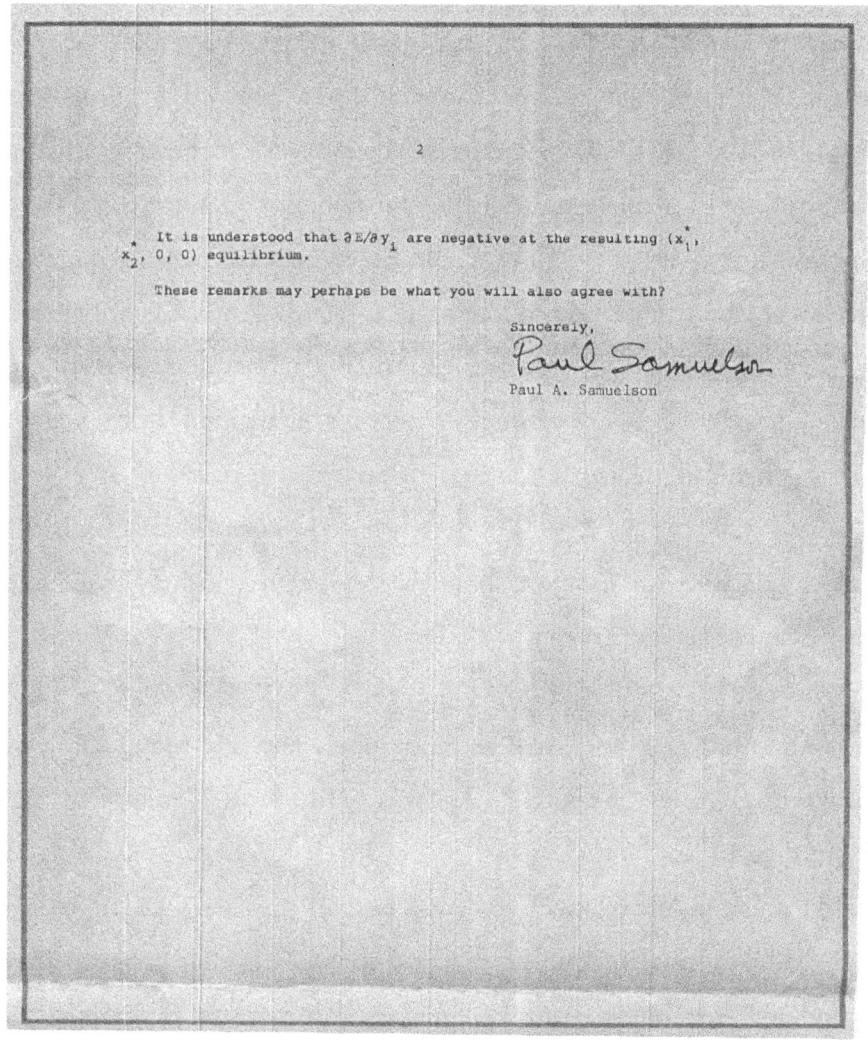

Figure 3. Samuelson's letter page 2

CHAPTER 4. ANDREAS HUYSSEN

What is most important to me remains my brother's *Udaipur Tinsmiths*, because it is such an important record of Abstract Expressionism's and Post Painterly Abstraction's forceful bid to be the standard of Modern and then Hypermodern art. Who would have thought that their repudiation would be recorded in a 1964 painting that might be the very first Postmodern painting, a full twenty years in advance of the 1980s decade of American Postmodern painting, which I describe in my essay, "Pynchon's Transition from Ethos-based Postmodernism to Late-Postmodern Stylistics," in *Style* 43.2 (Summer 2009): 194-214. The ethos-based postmodernism that I now associate with *Udaipur Tinsmiths* is, I believe, more substantive than that in the *Style* article.

My understanding of Postmodernism and its repudiation of Modernism goes back to Andreas Huyysen's "Mapping the Postmodern" in *New German Critique* 33 (Fall 1984): 5-52. What I didn't realize until relatively recently is that Huyssen's article builds the repudiation of modernist art, and particularly that promoted by Clement Greenberg. To my surprise, Huyssen cites Greenberg's name eight times in his article: page 23 line 20, page 23 line 23, page 26 line 30, page 26 line 33, page 26 line 34, page 26 line 35, page 26 line 37, and page 39 line 37. Although he puts Greenberg in the same category as Theodor W. Adorno, a well known German writer and sociologist, there is no mention of Adorno in John O'Brian's book on Greenberg, *Modernism with a Vengeance, 1957-1969*, and I will leave that extension for research by others.

Some of what Huyssen says about Greenberg relates to writings in the O'Brian book that I have already revealed in the present work:

> It is no longer the modernism of "the age of anxiety," the aesthetic and tortured modernism of a Kafka, a modernism of negativity and alienation, ambiguity and abstraction, the modernism of the closed and finished work of art. (Andreas Huyssen 39)

Indeed the Greenberg that we know from O'Brian's book is too self-confident to be anxious or tortured and has no interest in ambiguity. He does write about abstraction, but not in the sense of its being closed or finished. Huyssen continues:

> Rather it is a modernism of playful transgression, of an unlimited weaving of textuality, a modernism all confident in its rejection of representation and reality, in its denial of the subject, of history, and of the subject of history; a modernism quite dogmatic in its rejection of presence and in its unending praise of lacks and absences, deferrals and traces which produce, presumably, not anxiety but, in Roland Barthes' terms, *jouissance*, bliss. (Huyssen 39-40)

The reference to "playful transgression" seems apt—it would have turned off my brother—as does the allusion "to a modernism all confident in its rejection of representation and reality," which is the essence of what Greenberg rejects. There is no mention of Barthes in O'Brian's volume, and Huyssen's desire to add a European aspect to Greenberg's modernism seems misplaced. Huyssen could be understood as reassuring my brother when he writes that:

> We are not bound to *complete* [Greenberg's] project of modernity [… nor] necessarily have to lapse into irrationality or into some apocalyptic frenzy, the sense that art is not exclusively pursuing some telos of abstraction, non-representation and sublimity—all of this has opened up a host of possibilities for creative endeavors today. And in certain ways it has altered our views of modernism itself. (Huyssen 49).

Bill would have been skeptical, as would I have been, of this host of possibilities for creative endeavors today. Just leave aesthetic choice open. But the fact is that Greenberg's strategy triumphed. The art that he ratified became very valuable at auction. It held its popularity from the 1950s and 60s into the present. The St. Louis Art Museum can well celebrate its enormous success. I'm not sure that Huyssen had it right or that it would even have mattered had we begun to explore the contradictions and contingencies [in Greenberg's Modernism], its tensions and internal resistances to its own "forward" movement. [...] On the contrary, it [cast] a new light on it and appropriate[d] many of its aesthetic strategies and techniques inserting them and making them work in new constellations. What [never] became obsolete however are those codifications of modernism in critical discourse which, however, are based on [Greenberg's] teleological view of progress and modernization [, and which never actually] prepared the ground for that repudiation of modernism which goes by the name of the postmodern. (Huyssen 49)

EPILOGUE

Bill Kohn is gone; Clement Greenberg is gone. *Udaipur Tinsmiths*, the painting, lives on to inspire art lovers to recall a difficult, anguished, period of rejection in my brother's career. What of me? I am wrestling with thoughts of an easy death for myself. This may be the last book I have to write, and with it goes my imagined purpose in living. I have wrestled with the idea of speeding up the process of my dying. But no one likes it when I talk this way, and I am sensitive to my friends' and my sons' feelings that I should live out the days that my body has left. Ned Durham feels sure that I will not run out of interests in life. But he believes in a personal God, which I do not. If there is a personal God I reject him for the undeserved anguish, like that of the six-million Holocaust Jews, that he has allowed to happen in the world and continues to allow. But that's really beside the point; God has no meaning in my life. There is no external power that can interfere with human iniquity.

If I were dead, I would no longer need round-the-clock nursing, and the money I have managed to save would be available to my sons, as Martha and I always intended. I wish that a conversation could go on about helping people on the verge of dying to expire. But what are the facts? I have metatasized prostate cancer and may no longer be able to urinate on my own. This requires that I be equipped with a Foley catheter, which has high maintenance requirements. It has to be reinserted monthly under sterile conditions. It includes a storage bag for spent urine, which the patient has to monitor or have monitored for him as in my case. The spent urine must be disposed. In addition the patient has to drink fresh water to keep the urine flowing healthily. One is too busy trying to sustain the flow to think about dying. Sustaining the flow prevents dehydration. One could just give up, but then the body's organs would shut down. To die of dehydration is drawn out and painful. If suicide is ruled out, what is the natural way to die of metastasized prostate cancer? There are many possibilities for shutdown; the body can stop breathing, the heart can stop beating, the brain can stop controlling.

What is so bad about living longer than I would like? Most importantly, it is costly. I must pay to have nursing students and care givers throughout the long days and nights. But these are wonderful people and they deserve more than they are paid. Besides, I am the beneficiary of Medicare's generosity, and should be happy to pay for my care takers. Moreover, my wife insisted that we have long-term home-health-care insurance coverage, which pays a portion of the home nursing. I cannot argue that dying should be cost-free.

www.ingramcontent.com/pod-product-compliance
Lightning Source LLC
Chambersburg PA
CBHW070731180526
45167CB00004B/1701